Knowledge
MASTERS

OPTICAL ILLUSIONS

Written by
Duncan Muir

Published by
Alligator Books Limited
Gadd House, Arcadia Avenue
London N3 2JU

Printed in China

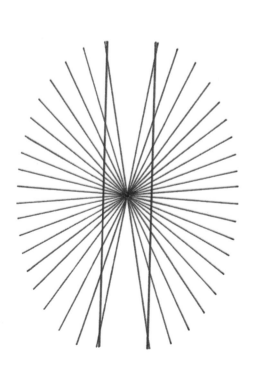

Contents

About this book

Your eyes can sometimes be tricked into seeing something that is not really there! An object might look different from how it actually is. This is an optical illusion.

You are surrounded by optical illusions every day. Pictures on a television screen and rainbows in the sky are both examples of optical illusions, one mechanical, the other natural. They are illusions because they do not really exist. People and objects are not actually inside your television and rainbows are merely a trick of the light.

This book will show you some of the many optical illusions that exist, and explain how they work. You can also try some out for yourself.

In the top right hand corner of this book there are a series of pictures. Carefully bend the book and quickly let the corner of each page flick through your fingers. The hammer will appear to move. The individual pictures move so fast that your brain is tricked into thinking that there is only one moving picture. Try this for yourself by drawing a figure in slightly different poses on each page of a drawing pad.

When your eyes are open light travels into them from the world outside. The source of the light could be the Sun, or a light bulb.

Before it enters your eyes, light reflects off objects that are in your **field of vision** – the things you can see.

Sometimes there is not much information for the brain to work with. It must use other information to understand what it is seeing. If you cover up the second of the two words below it is not so easy to see that the first word is FISH. Your brain fills in the gaps by using any other available information.

FISH FINGERS

There is a **blind spot** at the back of your eye where the optic nerve connects to the brain. It is an area which is insensitive to light.

The image on the **retina** is actually upside-down but your brain flips the image allowing you to see it the right way up.

<u>The eye</u>

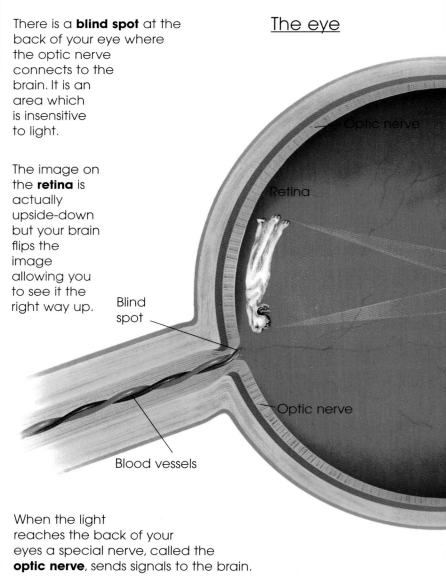

Optic nerve

Retina

Blind spot

Blood vessels

Optic nerve

When the light reaches the back of your eyes a special nerve, called the **optic nerve**, sends signals to the brain.

Even when your eyes are shut your brain still thinks it sees. When your eyes have been looking at a bright light or you have been staring hard at something, an **after-image** can stay at the back of your eye for some time. Try staring for a minute or two at the black cat, then close your eyes. You should see an image of the cat even though your eyes are closed.

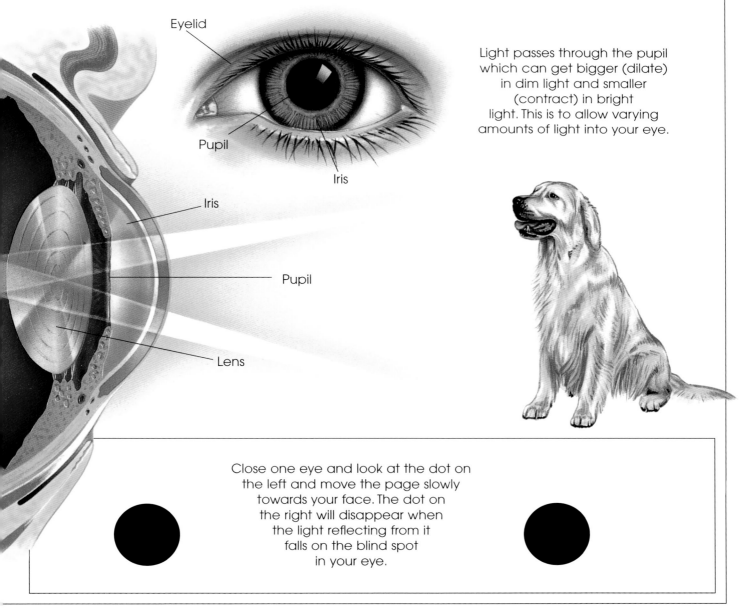

Eyelid

Pupil

Iris

Iris

Pupil

Lens

Light passes through the pupil which can get bigger (dilate) in dim light and smaller (contract) in bright light. This is to allow varying amounts of light into your eye.

Close one eye and look at the dot on the left and move the page slowly towards your face. The dot on the right will disappear when the light reflecting from it falls on the blind spot in your eye.

Simple lines and shapes can fool your brain. Phantom blobs can appear from nowhere and straight lines can seem to bend.

Try staring at the circle. You will find it hard to see a steady picture. Your eyes are being drawn to the centre of the circle where the black stripes get closer and closer together. The lines appear to 'interfere' with each other, producing a shadow effect around the circle. This is known as the **Mackay Effect**.

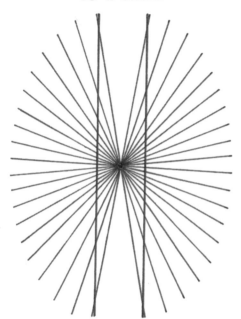

Here are some diagrams that will trick your eyes.

The unenclosed circles at the centres of the crossed lines seem to be brighter than the enclosed outlined circles.

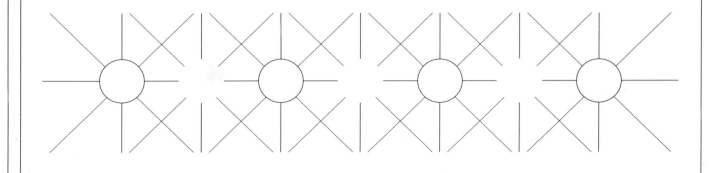

Stare at the black squares and you will see faint shaded blobs at the corners.

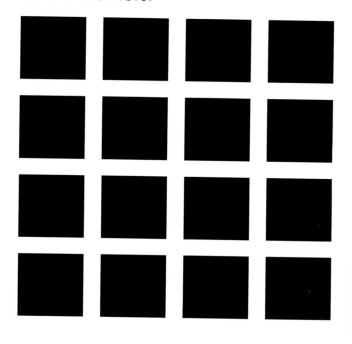

Stare at the white squares and pale blobs appear, again at the corners.

Which of these lines do you think is longest? A or B? In fact they are both the same length. Your eyes follow the direction of the arrows which makes your brain think one line is shorter than the other.

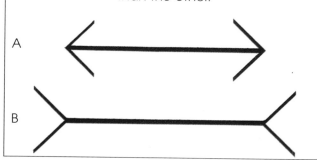

Parallel lines are lines that are the same distance apart, however long they are. Here, the parallel lines seem to curve away from each other.

The diagonal lines draw your eyes away from the horizontal lines, making them appear to bend.

Do the bricks in this wall seem as if they are being partly squashed? Although they are, in fact, all rectangles, they appear to be wedge-shaped. This interesting optical illusion only works when the lines between the bricks are brighter than the dark bricks and darker than the light bricks.

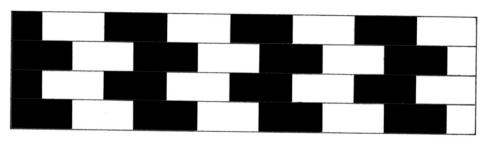

What is a three-dimensional image?

We live in three-dimensional space. This means we can move from side to side (one dimension), forwards and backwards (the second dimension) and we can jump up and down (the third dimension).

A flat sheet of paper has only two dimensions, but an object can be drawn so it looks three-dimensional.

This drawing of a cube appears to be a three-dimensional (3-D) shape, even though the paper it is printed on is only two-dimensional (2-D). The brain is being tricked into believing the lines form a 3-D figure.

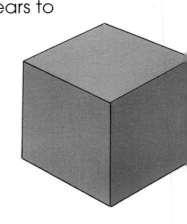

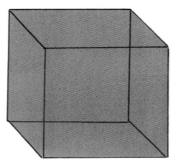

This type of cube is known as the **Necker cube**, named after the man who first drew it.

There is no way of knowing which is the front or back of the cube.

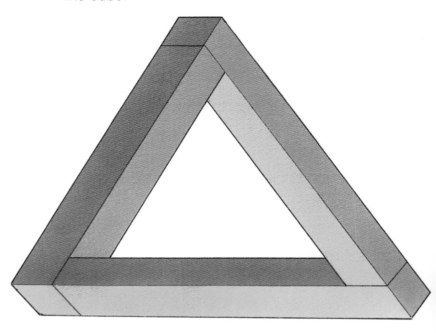

This 3-D triangle, sometimes called a **tribar**, appears to be a picture of a simple 3-D shape. However, on closer inspection it is clear that it could not exist in a real three-dimensional space!

Railway lines are parallel lines. However, a picture of a railway track disappearing into the distance shows the lines getting closer and closer together. This is called perspective. **Perspective** is used to show 3-D pictures in 2-D.

To learn the rules of perspective, artists sometimes paint what they see through a window on to the glass itself!

The Dutch artist **Maurits C Escher** produced amazing geometric drawings. Some are of buildings that at first glance appear quite normal, but would be quite impossible to build in real life.

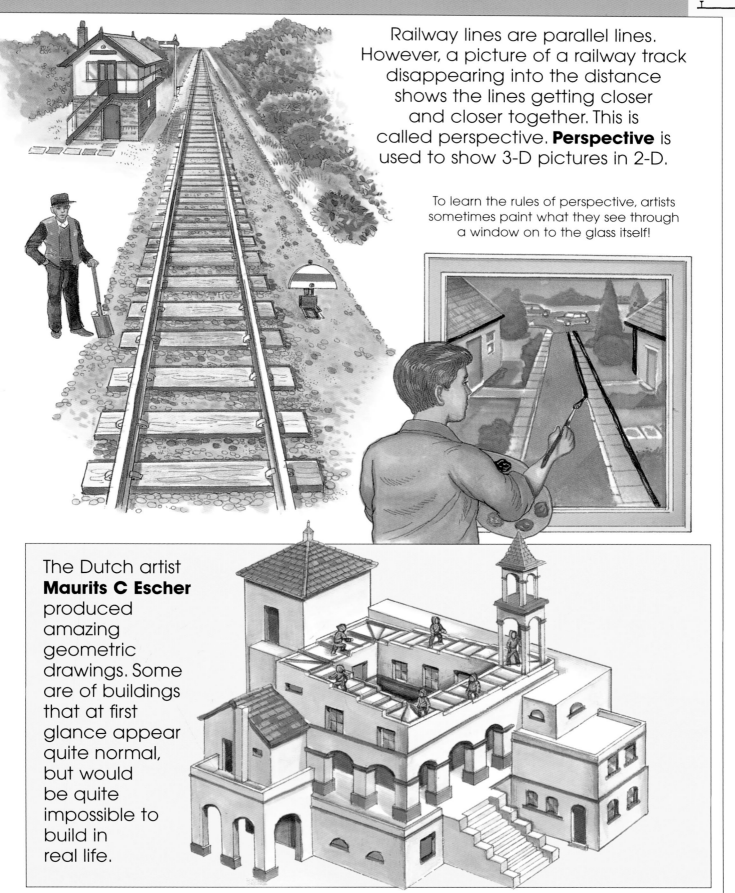

How does our brain compare sizes?

A mouse looks tiny when compared to a human, but compared to a flea it looks huge.

The brain always compares one thing with another to decide their size or position. However, these comparisons can often confuse the brain!

Clouds are a **scaled** phenomenon. This means it is impossible to tell how near or far away they are, as there is nothing to compare the clouds to in order to guess their size.

At a reading distance of 30 cm, the mouse and the elephant appear to be the same size. In real life, if the mouse (40 mm high) were in the foreground the elephant (three metres high) would have to be 32 metres behind the mouse to appear to be the same size.

A constellation is a group, or pattern, of stars. The Plough, part of the Ursa Major constellation, is made up of seven bright stars. When viewed from Earth they all appear to be the same distance away, but in fact some are much closer than others.

A light year is the distance light travels in a year. Light travels at 300,000 km per second, so a light year is around 9,460,000,000,000 km!

The closest star in the Plough to Earth is 60 light years away, the furthest is an amazing 110 light years away!

As the light from the furthest star in the Plough takes 110 years to reach us, it may not even be there any more and we would not realise. If the star had burnt out five years ago we would not be able to tell for another 105 years!

Which is the largest of the centre circles? They are both the same size! Your brain compared them with the circles that are surrounding them and decided that one was 'small' in comparison with other circles and the other was 'big'.

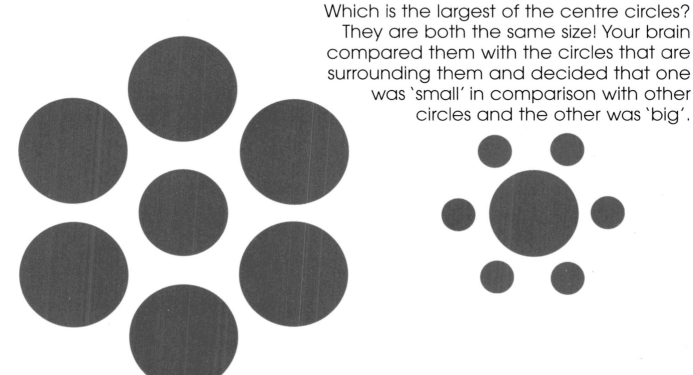
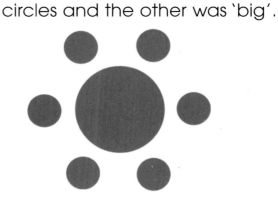

What is colour?

Light can be split into different colours. These colours are red, orange, yellow, green, blue and violet, and are called the spectrum.

Rainbows are a natural example of how sunlight can be split into the colours of the spectrum (see page 28).

You can try a simple experiment to see how the colours of the spectrum combine to make white light. Divide a card circle into six sections and colour the segments the colours of the spectrum. Push a pencil through the centre of the card. When you spin the pencil fast, the colours will blend together until they look white.

There are two sorts of cell in the human eye which are sensitive to light. They are shaped like **cones** and **rods**. The cones are sensitive to bright light and the colours red, blue and green. The rods are sensitive to dim light, but not colour.

Cone

Rod

The eye

Sometimes photographers use coloured **filters** on the camera lens. The filter blocks some of the colours in the spectrum and can make photographs look very dramatic.

Using a yellow filter makes blue sky look darker and makes white clouds stand out more.

Stare at the red square in the centre of the red and white checkered pattern for about a minute. Now stare at the white square at its right. The white square will seem to change to a faint cyan (a shade of blue).

When two colours can combine to produce white light, they are said to be **complementary** colours.

The cones in your retinas have become tired of taking in the red light. So, for a while, your eyes will ignore it. The colour produced by the rest of the light is cyan. Cyan is the complementary colour to red.

If a person cannot see some colours, they are called **colour blind**. Colour blindness is 20 times more common in men than in women.

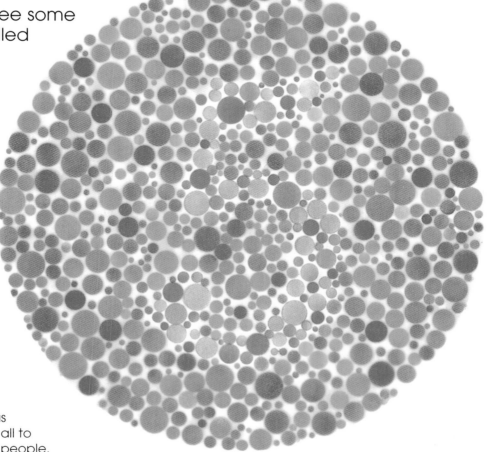

Tests like this are used to see if people are red-green colour blind.

Colour blindness is not serious and makes no difference at all to the day-to-day lives of most people.

How are cinema films made?

Cinema films are often called 'movies'. However, when you watch a 'movie' you simply see a series of still pictures shown quickly one after another. Each picture or **frame**, is slightly different from the previous one so an illusion of movement is created.

Sometimes when watching a film or the television, you might see a car wheel apparently spinning the wrong way. This happens when the position of the wheel's spokes in each frame makes it easier for the brain to think that the wheel is moving slowly backwards than very fast forwards.

A technique often used in nature films is **time-lapse photography**.

Individual pictures are taken of an object every day, and are then joined in sequence to make a film. In this way, a week in the life of a plant can be seen in a matter of seconds. This is an extreme form of fast-motion.

In the 19th century, before moving film was invented, you could have seen simple animation with a toy called a **zoetrope**.

The spinning drum had evenly spaced slits cut into it. Through each slit you could see a small image that was drawn slightly differently to the one next to it. Spinning the drum let you see one image after another, creating the illusion of movement.

Television pictures are made up of many tiny luminescent dots that form several lines across the screen. The dots are constantly changed from top to bottom, producing 25 frames every second. As the images change so quickly they appear to be moving.

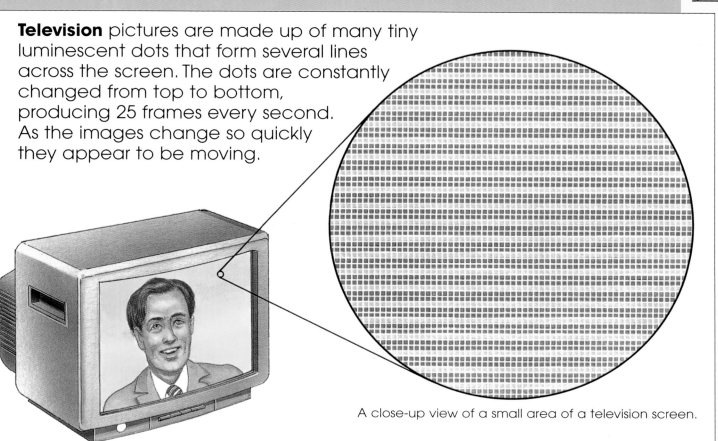

A close-up view of a small area of a television screen.

Animated films or **cartoons** work like normal films, except that between each frame the picture, or model, is changed slightly, either by hand or on a computer.

Some animated films use models made from modelling clay. The models must be changed slightly between each frame. It can take up to two years to make a 30-minute film using animated models.

15

As your eyes are about six centimetres apart you see things from two slightly different angles. This is called **binocular vision**.

Your brain has two views of the same thing to deal with, but it cleverly combines the two views so that your mind sees in 3-D. This is **stereo vision**.

The field of vision is the area in which you can see things without moving your eyes. A fly has hundreds of eyes, giving it a very wide field of vision. This makes it very difficult for a predator to sneak up on it, or a human to swat it!

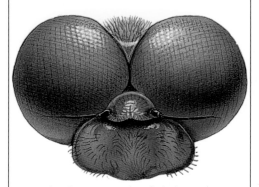

A close-up of a fly's head.

Stereo vision allows people to judge how far away an object is. This is called **spatial awareness**. It is much harder for your brain to judge the position of an object when it only sees the object through one eye (from one angle). You can try this yourself by throwing and catching a ball, or picking a ball up off the floor, when you have one eye closed.

Put the tips of your index fingers together and hold them about 20 cm away from your eyes. Relax your eyes or look at something a few feet in front of you. You will see that the ends of your fingers appear to overlap. A sausage-like object appears between your fingers.

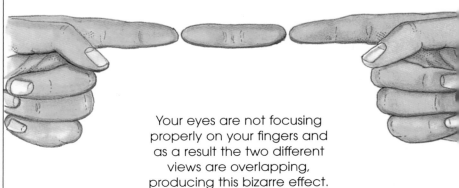

Your eyes are not focusing properly on your fingers and as a result the two different views are overlapping, producing this bizarre effect.

Each eye has a different view of the same
object. If you close your left eye and point at
a small object in the distance, and then
close your right eye and look with the left,
you will no longer be pointing at the object.

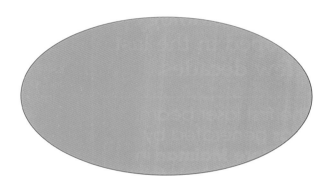

You can see
3-D pictures
and 3-D films
by wearing
special
glasses with
one red and
one green
lens.

Two slightly different
views of the picture
are drawn on top of
each other. Each view
can only be seen
through one lens of
the coloured glasses.
As each eye has a
different picture, your
brain then combines
them to produce a
3-dimensional picture.

Holograms and stereograms are two ways of representing a 3-D image.

When lit correctly, a hologram can make a 2-D image appear to be in 3-D.

They are both created using technology developed in the last few decades.

The first laser beam was generated by **Theodore Maiman** in 1960 using a flash tube and a ruby crystal.

A hologram is created using **laser light**. The laser beam is split in two. One half of it is reflected from the object on to the film material. The other half is directed straight on to the film without reflecting from the object. When the hologram film is lit in a certain way, a 3-dimensional picture can be seen.

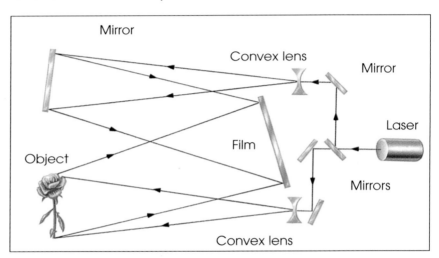

Laser light waves are coherent – they are the same length and go up and down together. Holograms can only be made using laser light as the process requires regular light waves. Unlike laser light, ordinary light waves are highly irregular and therefore useless for the job.

A **stereogram** is a computer-generated picture that seems, at first, to be a random pattern of coloured dots and squiggles. But if you look at a stereogram in a particular way, a seemingly 3-D image emerges from within the pattern.

To see the stereogram try focusing on a point beyond the stereogram. It is not as easy as it sounds. Focus and then relax your eyes.

A 3-D picture is hidden in the scattered dots of a stereogram (the answer is at the bottom of the page). A computer is used to work out where the dots should be positioned. The dots make up two images of the same shape – one for each eye. When you stare at the stereogram in the right way, your brain mixes the two images and magically recognizes the shapes in the picture.

Answer: It is a picture of a dinosaur.

These days most films are full of incredible special effects, which can be created using computers.

Film makers have always used visual illusions, even in the early days of cinema, over 100 years ago. Then illusions were based upon the successful techniques used on stage.

Early comedy film makers like **Max Sennet** and **Charlie Chaplin** used simple filming techniques to produce hilarious results. Although their special effects do not seem very convincing compared with modern techniques, they were revolutionary at the time.

One of the earliest special effects used in the theatre was **Pepper's Ghost**. A large mirror, hidden beneath the stage, reflected the figure of an actor on to a large piece of glass at the front of the stage. As the glass was invisible on the darkened stage, the audience saw a transparent phantom appearing in front of them!

In the 1902 film, *A Trip to the Moon*, film makers used trick photography to show a rocket crashing into the moon.

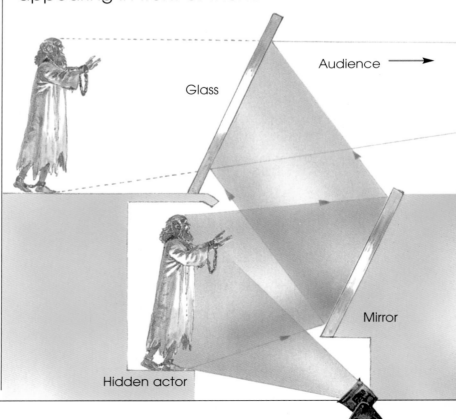

Audience

Glass

Mirror

Hidden actor

A technique that is used a lot in film and television is **superimposition**. Two film sequences are shown at the same time. This gives the illusion that the actor is appearing twice in the same shot.

On television, superimposition is often done using **Colour Separation Overlay**. Two videos, or the pictures from two cameras, are shown at the same time. Wherever the colour blue appears on the first picture, the second picture shows through.

With the help of computers it is possible to create almost any visual effect you could wish for on television or film. A picture can be stored **digitally** as trillions of binary numbers (ones and zeros). Computer software can perform complicated calculations with the stored numbers to produce spectacular effects.

Morphing is an effect where one object can appear to be smoothly transformed into another.

Most magic tricks are optical illusions that require years of practice. Magicians, or illusionists as they are sometimes known, are skilled at deceiving the eye.

Magicians use **sleight of hand** to deceive their audience. This means they can cleverly move a small object, such as a coin, without anyone noticing.

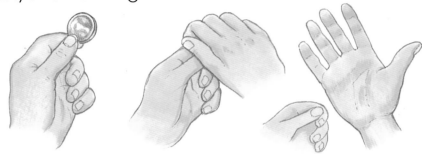

Palming is a method of holding playing cards or coins, without the audience seeing. It takes a lot of practice to make hand movements look natural while concealing an object.

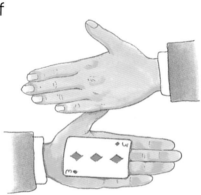

David Copperfield is one of the most famous magicians in the world today. One of his most successful illusions is when he appears to fly around the stage.

To aid sleight of hand and palming, magicians try to distract the audience's attention, often by waving a 'magic' **wand**.

Drop a one pence coin into an empty drinking glass. Pour water into the glass and the coin will appear to become a two pence coin!

Make sure your audience only sees the coin through the side of the glass by holding your hand around the rim.

The water distorts the audience's view of the coin making it appear larger than it really is.

Hold two coins between your index fingers. Rub the two coins quickly together and it will appear that there are now three coins.

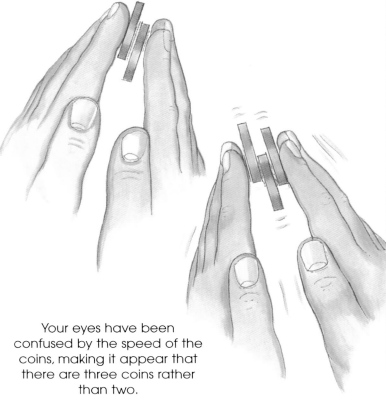

Your eyes have been confused by the speed of the coins, making it appear that there are three coins rather than two.

Light can bounce and bend. This is known as reflection (bouncing) and refraction (bending).

Light reflects from a mirror and refracts on entering and leaving water, sometimes producing amazing effects.

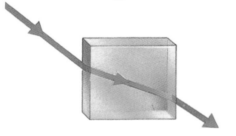

When light passes from air to water, it refracts. **Refracted light** distorts images. If you stand in the shallow end of a swimming pool and look down at your legs, they appear to be much shorter and stubbier than when you are out of the water. This is not because they have shrunk, it is because light is bent, or refracted.

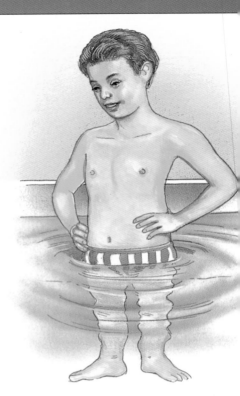

A simple experiment to see how light refracts can be tried using a straw and a glass of water. Dip the straw in the glass of water and view it from different angles. The light bends on contact with the water, distorting the image of the straw.

The famous artist Leonardo da Vinci did not want other people to copy his ideas. So he sometimes used **mirror writing** when making his notes. Mirror writing can only be read if it is held up to a mirror.

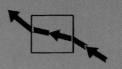

A **concave** mirror curves inwards, like the bowl of a spoon. Light that reflects off it **converges** (comes together). The light focuses at a point in front of the mirror. After it has focused, the light **diverges** (separates).

The reflection in a concave mirror is upside down.

A **convex** mirror curves outwards, like the back of a spoon. It produces a small upright image, but also has a wide field of view. This means it shows things to the sides which a normal mirror would not reflect.

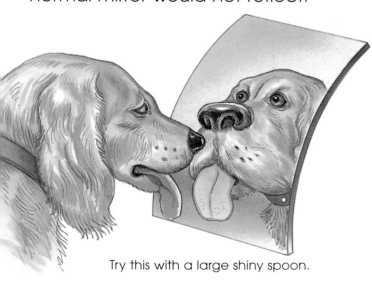

Try this with a large shiny spoon.

You may have seen weird images of yourself in a **Hall of Mirrors** at a fairground. The mirrors are curved so that some parts are concave and some are convex.

If the light meets your eye before it focuses, you see a magnified image of your face. If the light meets your eye after the focal point, you see an upside down image of your face.

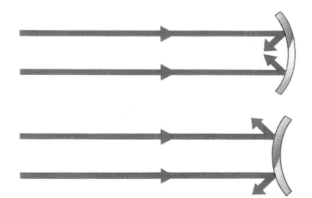

How are optical illusions used?

Optical illusions are often entertaining, but they can also be very useful.

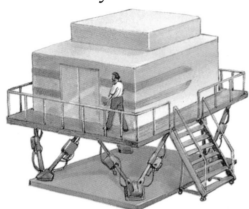

Deceiving our eyes can allow us to practise dangerous activities – but without the danger.

Pilots who fly large modern aeroplanes have to be very well trained in order to prevent accidents. Pilots can practise their skills using specially built machines called **flight simulators**.

Simulators are built to be exactly like the cockpit of the plane. Large computer screens display a realistic moving picture of what the pilots would see if they were really flying the plane. The computer-generated pictures respond to the controls as the pilot manipulates them.

Fashion designers use optical illusions when designing clothes.

Wearing clothes with vertical stripes makes you look taller and slimmer.

Horizontally striped clothing (hoops) can make you look shorter and fatter.

Wearing all black can also make you appear slimmer.

Using a design method called **Computer Aided Design**, architects can design a house, and see inside the rooms using the 3-D image on the computer screen. House buyers can be shown around the house as if it was already built.

Landscape architects can design a garden to make it look bigger than it really is. If a path gradually becomes narrower as it gets further away, the garden will look longer.

If you looked down the garden your brain would assume that the path was the same width from one end to the other and, therefore, that the end of the garden was further away.

In some countries, the stretch of road approaching a roundabout is striped with **yellow lines**, which get closer and closer together towards the roundabout. This creates the illusion that vehicles are travelling very quickly and encourages drivers to brake earlier to reach a safer speed.

Some optical illusions occur naturally. They are all around us.

Strange illusions appear in the sky, certain animals can blend into their surroundings, or look like something completely different.

On some clear days at sunset the sun will appear to turn bright green for a few seconds. This is called the **green flash**.

WARNING:
NEVER LOOK DIRECTLY AT THE SUN!

A **rainbow** is a natural optical illusion that can appear when sunlight reflects off raindrops.

The light from the sun is bent as it travels through the drops. The different colours that make up white light do not bend at the same angle, so they are split into the six colours of the spectrum. Although it can appear as if there are seven colours in a rainbow, most experts agree there are only six.

On sunny days, pools of water seem to appear on the road. This is known as a **mirage**. The light has been refracted by the rising hot air close to the ground. The expanding hot air also makes the light shimmer, giving an overall effect of blue rippling water.

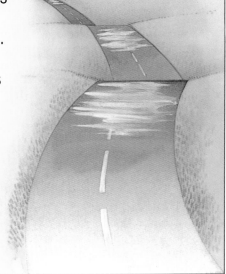

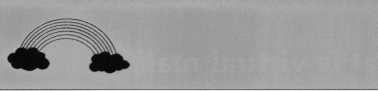

Peacock butterflies scare off predators with the vividly coloured circles on each wing. These look like a pair of ferocious eyes.

Some animals have evolved ways of hiding themselves from other creatures. They use **camouflage**. A lion has sandy coloured fur to make it hard to see in the long dry grass.

Zebra, which might be a lion's prey, are marked with irregular black and white stripes. The stripes make it hard for the lions to tell one zebra from another in a large herd.

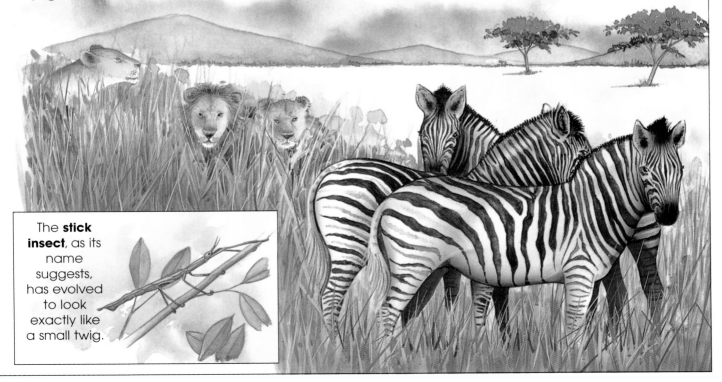

The **stick insect**, as its name suggests, has evolved to look exactly like a small twig.

Imagine wandering through a world that does not exist, or catching a ball that is not there. It is all possible with virtual reality.

Virtual Reality is anything that seems to exist but does not. A painting you might do of an imaginary house is virtual reality! The house only exists in the painting. With modern computers we can experience **Interactive Virtual Reality**. Interactive means it responds to things that you do.

Virtual Reality computer programs can create imaginary landscapes that seem as real as the view you might see from the window of a train. Computer programmers use mathematical formulae to generate very realistic landscapes that move with you through this virtual world.

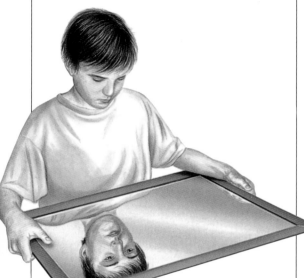

If you look into a **mirror**, you can see a virtual world behind your reflection. Try holding a mirror horizontally in front of you while you walk from room to room. It seems like you are walking on the ceiling.

WARNING:
BE VERY CAREFUL IF YOU DO THIS, AS IT COULD BE VERY DANGEROUS

There are various items of equipment that can be used for exploring virtual reality. The most well known is the **headset**. In front of the eyes are two tiny TV screens that give you a 3-D view of the computer generated landscape. Some more expensive headsets change the view as you move your head up and down or from side to side.

A **VR glove** contains sensors that can detect the movements of your fingers. Soon gloves will have sensors that make it seem as if you can actually feel virtual objects, objects that do not really exist.

Index